HOW TO
STOP FARTING IN 10 DAYS
(or your money back)

Turnbull & Willoughby

Publishers

HOW TO
STOP FARTING IN 10 DAYS
(or your money back)

Dr. Herbert K. Poltweed

Illustrated by Tom Olcese

First published January, 1987

10   9   8   7   6   5   4   3   2   1

Manufactured in the United States of America

ISBN : 0-943084-51-2

Published by
Turnbull & Willoughby Publishers
44 E. Superior Street
Chicago, IL 60611

To my long time good friend and associate Mike Mervis who
is always complaining that nobody ever dedicates a book to him.

Table of Contents

A NOTE FROM THE AUTHOR
Why Someone Bought This Book For You.

Dear Reader:

It occurs to me that you may be wondering why anyone would buy this book for *you.* The answer, if I may be blunt, is simple: You fart too much (worst of all you seem to enjoy doing it) and the person who bought you this book wishes you would stop.

Don't try to look surprised. Do you think for a moment that your extragastrointestinal activities have gone unnoticed? Have you ever wondered why, when you enter the room everyone suddenly leaves while wildly waving their arms? Why cats and dogs roll over and play dead whenever you're near? Why friends and relatives rush to shut off their pilot lights when you arrive?

Noooo...you've never *wondered.* You've known all along? So don't try to act surprised. It won't work.

But don't feel bad. Simply because someone thinks you fart too much and bought you this book is no reason to feel rejected.

Just as farting is nature's way of telling you that your intestinal tract is having a good time, the gift of this book is simply a friend or loved one's way of telling you that you are an evil smelling, ill mannered and disgusting slob!

Just kidding. Actually, if you will stop and think for a moment, you will feel quite good about receiving this book. If people didn't enjoy you enough to want to spend time with you, why would they be offering to help cure you of your disgusting habit?

Dr. H.K. Poltweed

Lesson Number One "FART SOUNDS"

FAMOUS CARTOONISTS SCHOOL

* Silent But Deadly

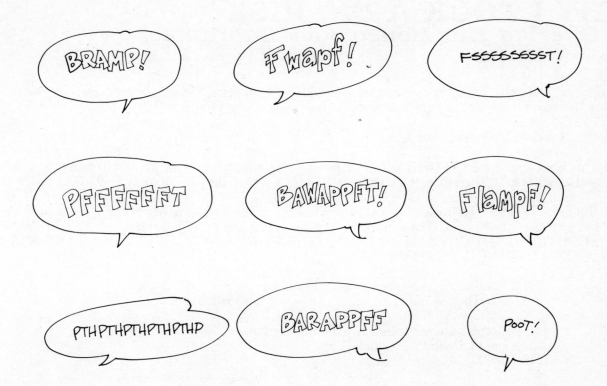

WHY I TOOK A *BIG* RISK:
(By Offering This Money Back Guarantee)

"Big risk," you say. "So a few disgruntled individuals might demand their money back. So what? You're going to make millions of dollars selling this revolutionary new program."

"Not so" I respond. Consider the reality:

(1) This book sells for $5.95 (well worth the price, I might add, for all the joy it will bring to your friends and loved ones). Therefore, if a customer asks for a refund they will expect $5.95 BACK.

(2) But *I don't get* $5.95 a book. I've got to wholesale this book to book stores and gift stores and they have to make *their* profit. For the sake of argument let's say I sell it to retailers for $3.00. WAIT A MINUTE...I ONLY GET $3.00 AND I GOTTA REFUND SIX BUCKS? LET'S TAKE A CLOSE LOOK AT WHAT COULD HAPPEN:

  - I sell 4 million books (conservative estimate)
    at $3.00. That equals........................... 12 Million Dollars

  - 47 customers are not satisfied with my program
    and want their whole six bucks back
    (47 x $6.00)... $282.00
                                                      _____

                    My gross profit only $11,999,728.00

- But wait another minute! You forget I have to
print the book (and you'd be surprised how ex-
pensive this can be) 4,000,000 books at $ .39 each.
That equals..,.............................. ($1,600,000.00)

My real profit only $10,399,728.00

   Now, you may think this is a reasonable profit but I want you to remember this program represents 15 *years* of dedication and hard work...15 years of rejection, loneliness, ridicule and shame. That works out to *less than* $700,000 per year!

   I think now you can understand why I made it virtually impossible for anyone to collect on my famous money back guarantee. If you wish a refund you must try *every* step of my program. If your farting does not stop entirely in 10 days (and you are still alive), simply obtain a certified letter from your family doctor stating that you have indeed attempted each and every one of the Poltweed steps. Send this along with a small processing fee of $6.25 and your refund will be forthcoming.

Sincerely,

Dr. Herbert K. Poltweed

P.S. If you're still not feeling sorry for me regarding the money back guarantee keep in mind I never even
      added in the cost of buying 4 million of those stupid clothespins and sticking them to each and every book!!

Olfactory Inhibiting Device indeed!!

WHY IS IT SO DIFFICULT TO STOP?
Teaching Old Dogs New Tricks

I'm sure you are sick and tired of everybody you've ever known constantly making subtle comments about how they wish you would cease and desist farting. I know most of them are just "Do-gooders" and often they are pleasant about it but it *does* get tiring.

When I was young, for example, my dear mother would often look at me lovingly and say, "You are the most evil smelling, disgusting, rude and obnoxious child any mother could have ever wished to have. In fact, I am so embarrased and ashamed of you that I wish you had never been born! And you have an ugly nose too!!"

Of course this would always hurt me deeply and certainly caused me to carry emotional scars throughout my life. All through my youth I felt unloved and unwanted. My dream was to someday get a good education, start a career save lots of money and be able to afford a good nose job.

DON'T PEOPLE REALIZE WE WOULD QUIT IF WE COULD?

My mother, like my other relatives and friends, simply didn't realize that I wasn't *trying* to be difficult. I would have *liked* to stop but couldn't seem to. Of course there are some individuals who couldn't care less about the feeling of others and continue to pass gas to their heart's content but this is not generally the case. The vast majority of us would dearly love to stop but *it's just not as easy as most people think!*

With this thought in mind I spent the early part of my medical research looking into the question of why it is so difficult to stop. I was astounded by my findings!! After reading this you will have plenty of ammunition to use when people scream at you: "Why don't you stop farting you disgusting slob?!"

TRUE FACT

The average person's
intestinal tract looks
like this.

The habitual farter's
intestinal tract looks
like this.

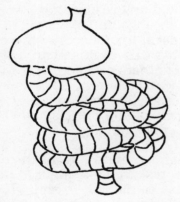

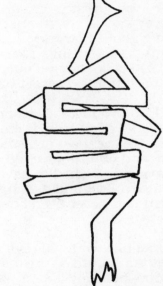

And *that's* why it's so difficult for some of
us to stop.

For those of you who require a more detailed explanation, I'll do my best to put it in layman's terms (this might be somewhat difficult for me because, as a trained physician I'm used to big, complicated Latin words and indecipherable sentences).

In the average guy's (or gal's) innards there are all these slimy tubes which squiggle and twist every which way somewhere near the stomach. When food is swallowed it mixes with stomach acid and then slips and slides through this slimy mess of tubes and *no problems* occur.

But the habitual farter was born with innards that make all these weird *right angle* turns! There is never a soft curve like this ⌒⌒⌒ *All* of the turns are 90° like this ⌐ !!

As a result, the food and acid mixture can't slip and slide through. Every time it hits a turn it slams into the wall of the tube, bounces off and slides on to the next turn where it bumps into the wall again.

Well, needless to say, all of this slamming and bumping is pretty hard on our friend the food/acid mixture. It tends to jiggle it all around and shake it up pretty good and this releases billions of fart molucules which have to escape *somewhere*.

And that's how it works.

There. You have it. The true story. (If you mention this to your doctor and he gives you a strange look, don't lose confidence in my explanation. It's just that he is probably surprised to hear such a complicated physiological explanation expressed in layman's terms).

ISN'T IT TIME YOU STOPPED?
Everyone Else Thinks So

O.K.. Enough is enough! You've had your fun. Isn't it about time you stopped farting? You *know* that deep down inside you've been lying to yourself every time you say "nobody really notices". Come on now. Admit it. Face facts. You really *are* a disgusting slob and what's more...*everyone* around you *knows* it!

There is a common notion among farters that their habit is not offensive and is actually condoned by those around them. I conducted some scientific research into this area in an effort to get habitual farters to face reality.

THE POLTWEED EXIT POLL

So you think nobody notices? So you think nobody cares? Well have I got news for you! After interviewing over 1,000 habitual farters and 1,000 of their closest friends and relatives I discovered some subtle differences of opinion which you might like to take into consideration.

Habitual Farter's Cherished Belief	Response from their Friends and Relatives
"Nobody really notices"	"Like Hell!"
"Mine don't smell"	"You got to be kidding!"
"Mine don't smell bad"	"Aggghhh!!"

As you can plainly see, there are some minor discrepancies in the beliefs of the farter and the non-farter. Why do these discrepancies exist? Well, I have another of the famous Poltweed explanations for you.

MIRROR, MIRROR ON THE WALL

I was originally going to call this section "Try To Understand That Everyone Thinks You Are A Disgusting Slob But You". But I didn't think too many of my readers wanted to hear about that so I tricked you with a clever headline.

Now that I have your attention I know you'll read on to discover why farters hold these ridiculously stupid beliefs about themselves. Here we go.....

When people look in the mirror they believe that is what they look like to others. But when they see themselves on TV or in a photograph they always exclaim, "I don't look like *that*!" Or when they hear their voice on a tape recorder they say, "Is *that* how I sound!?"

Now, are you ready for how I'm going to make the connection between mirrors, tape recorders and farting? Well here it is.

Just as we don't hear or see ourselves as others do...we also don't *smell* ourselves as others do. And this is especially true in the case of the not-so-delicate aroma of the average fart. Over the years I've had hundreds of patients say to me, "I sure do feel sorry for other people. Their farts smell *so bad*. But I'm lucky. Mine are really innocuous. In fact they smell kind of *good*."

Well I have news for you buddy. *Everybody* believes that about their *own* farts. Open your eyes and ears for a change! (as opposed to other parts of your anatomy). Aren't you getting the message?!... *Nobody* likes (or can even stand) the odors and disgusting sounds *you* are emitting.... except you. And....you....don't... count.

ABOUT THE AUTHOR
Is He Qualified?

Certainly if you are going to attempt to follow the medical recommendations contained in my famous 10 day program, you should have the utmost confidence in me as a qualified doctor. Knowing this is a legitimate concern I will attempt to give you a brief summary of my qualifications and of the events which lead to my breakthrough in this field.

The good news is that I attended 12 different medical schools including Harvard, Stanford, University of Michigan and Penn State. At these various universities I perfected my anti-fart theories, prepared papers on the etiquette of farting, and generally made a nuisance of myself.

While other students were overly concerned with pouring over textbooks and taking exams I was unjustly accused of taking my studies lightly while I attempted to develop my theories.

The bad news, as you may have guessed, is that I was thrown out of 11 different medical schools including Harvard, Stanford, University of Michigan and Penn State before finally receiving a degree with high honors from the University of Eastern Bermuda Islands State (after being thrown out of Harvard, I went in search of the origins of the Bermuda Onion which I mistakenly thought originated in those islands and discovered a University willing to support my studies).

I must admit I am still somewhat miffed at the schools which threw me out. Perhaps all of the negative publicity had something to do with it but that's part of science! The Penn State incident, during which I inadvertently fed fatal doses of black beans to white mice, caused quite a stink, however, the most unfortunate accident of all, and the one which led to my seeking refuge in Bermuda, occurred at the Michigan State University medical labs in the early 60's. An unfortunate undergraduate

volunteer by the name of C.J. Pratt met with an untimely death while participating in the early equipment testing for the Very Strong Cork Technique. (Reader: Please note this technique has been greatly improved since that time).

Little was heard of me in the years immediately following the "Pratt Incident" for I went into virtual seclusion at my new home in Bermuda. I have just recently emerged from hiding confident that my revolutionary new program will fully vindicate me.

———————————

Asked why he coined such a ridiculous name for such a serious program, Dr. Poltweed responded: "Over the years I've ordered so many Ginzu knives and rock and roll collections (and never sent anything back), the "Ten Days or Your Money Back" title seemed just right."

ALL ABOUT YOUR NEW O.I.D.
Patent Pending

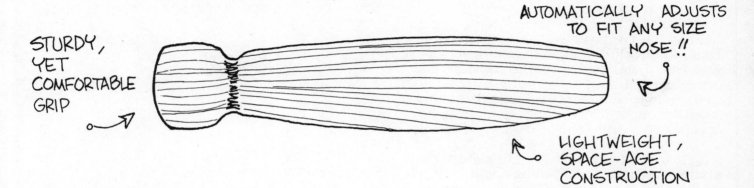

STURDY, YET COMFORTABLE GRIP

AUTOMATICALLY ADJUSTS TO FIT ANY SIZE NOSE !!

LIGHTWEIGHT, SPACE-AGE CONSTRUCTION

As the recipient of this book you are now the proud possessor of one of my legendary Olfactory Inhibiting Devices (OID) which should be attached to each book sold. (On occasion, books do reach the intended recipient without the OID attached but this is not, I repeat, NOT my fault or the fault of my illustrious publisher. I can best explain by asking you to consider what would happen if some publisher decided to sell a book about diamond mining and affixed a 10 carat diamond to each book. Aside from going broke, that publisher would be faced with countless complaints about books reaching the market without diamonds. Let's face it. Any time something extremely valuable is affixed to a product like a book, the manufacturer is taking the chance that some jerk will rip it off).

WHAT'S IN A NAME??

When I finally perfected my OID I ran into a legal problem which actually has nothing to do with stopping farting but I'm sure you would like to hear about it anyway.

"Now that I've invented this fantastic device", I said to myself, "What shall I name it?" Well, I was sure it was going to be an international sensation so I wanted the word "International" in the name. And, since it limits the ability to smell I thought "Unsmelling" would also be appropriate. And finally, "Device," of course.

It all seemed simple to me but my attorneys started screaming and yelling about how I'd get hit with thousands of lawsuits from female users who might use this device improperly.

I didn't understand but went along anyway and the International Unsmelling Device ultimately became known as the O.I.D., Olfactory Inhibiting Device. Lawyers!!!!

OLFACTORY INHIBITING DEVICE
(HOW TO USE THE POLTWEED O.I.D.)

The fact is, YOU will not be using it at all!!
The way things normally work is:

1) You receive a beautifully gift-wrapped package.

2) You say, "For meeee??".

3) You open the package and discover this book and you try to look confused.

4) Everyone around you laughs derisively, points at you and says, "Peeerrfeect gift!".

5) There is a mad dash by everyone within range to rip the OID off the book and quickly clamp it securely to their nose because...

6) ...You get so excited about recieving such a nice present that you start farting (of course).

MEN VS. WOMEN:
Who Farts More?

Actual scientific studies dating back to the early 1800's prove conclusively that dogs fart more than both men and women (or at least they get blamed the most), but that is not the question. . .

This gender problem has always intrigued me and, as part of my early university studies I sent questionnaires to 50,000 men and 50,000 women hoping to solve this age-old question. The questionnaires were straightforward:

Question #1)
Are you a Man?_____ Women?_____
Question #2)
Do you fart? _____

I was sure I had made an astounding discovery: 97.83% of all men surveyed admitted to farting but only *one percent* of the women did!!

But. . . all of those years at all of those medical schools taught me not to jump to conclusions. I pulled out the "never fart" responses from the women and reviewed them carefully. There it was!! . . .
The clue was in Question #14.

Question #14 : Did you lie when answering Question #2?

_____   _____
Yes   No

Fully 100% of the women who answered NO when asked if they farted had lied!! The new results looked like this:

	Quest. Sent	Say They Fart	Lied About It	Actually Fart	% of Total
Men	50,000	48,917	0	48,917	97.8%
Women	50,000	553	49,922	52,122	104.2%

Now the results are finally conclusive. There is simply no disputing real scientific evidence. More women fart than men! They just don't have the guts to admit it! How disgusting!!!

Footnote:
There is one small point in favor of the ladies. Question #42 asked "How many times a day do you fart?" The average for men was 46 times per day while the average for women was only $1^1/2$ times per day. So, while more women fart than do men, men do fart more. (Unless, of course, the gals lied again!)

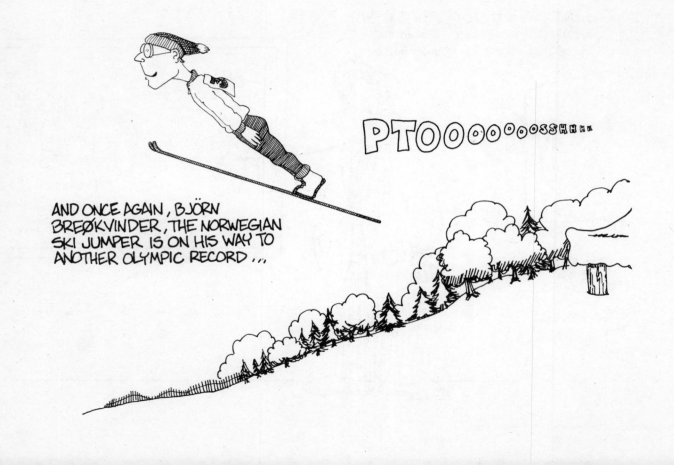

HISTORICAL METHODS
(And Why They Didn't Work)

During yet another of my periods of intensive studies I discovered that the problem of humans emitting foul smelling gasses has existed throughout known history. Although "legitimate" scientists are sure that the fart problem existed as early as 1654 a.d., it is my firm belief that it actually dates back as far as the Neanderthal period, 1087 b.s. (But, of course, nobody pays any attention to *me*.)

Sometimes the "legitimate scientific community" gives me a royal pain in the you-know-what. *They* can turn up the flimsiest of evidence to support their theories and end up on the cover of *Time* magazine. But just because I'm considered somewhat of a maverick, even when I turn up indisputable evidence, I can't even get a page 28 story in the Arlington Heights Daily Herald!

You think I'm kidding? Well, you be the judge as to whether the evidence I uncovered in Northwestern Arizona is *indisputable* or not.

Scientists studying ancient cave drawings discovered something like this and everyone agrees that the inhabitants of this period used spears

And when they find a drawing like this they immediately assume that they used the spears to hunt wild game.

But when *I* discover indisputable evidence such as *this*, do I get any respect? Nooooo!

My study of recent history has taught me
than man has endeavored to rid himself of
this bad habit on a continuing basis. He has
failed miserably in his attempts as he has had
with other serious problems such as war,
pestilence, famine and the common cold.
(That is, until *I* came along).

We, in the medical profession are progres-
sing however. In medieval times people
accused of emitting excessive gas were given
a "trial by fire" and burned at the stake.
Their accusers believed if the flames erupted
in a beautiful ball of blue flame it proved their
accusations were correct. Sometimes they
were right and sometimes they were wrong.
But when they were right, the sky would
light up for miles around and everyone would
gather around in awe.

Although modern methods are more
humane they have met with no more success.
Following are a few of the more up to date
methods both my colleagues and I have exper-
imented with.

PERMANANT SURGICAL RELIEF
(Is there a doctor in the house?)

I know what you're thinking. "Oh no, surgery. That sounds serious." Well, don't worry. Remember, I'm on *your* side, I want to *help* you with your problem and give you the benefit of my vast medical experience but, above all, I want to see you solve your problem in a manner which is as easy on you and as painless as possible.

Surgery works. Of that fact I am certain. Oh, I could tell you the stories about my early surgical experiments while in medical school!! Ah...those were the days...stitching up all those little white mice and then keeping them on diets of enchilladas and beer...every once in a while one of them would explode until I got the procedure down pat...but the really *great* fun was when one of those little rascals "sprung a leak" shall we say and took off like a balloon with a leak...bumping off the walls and the ceiling while emitting a constant buzzing sound until it ran out of gas. Ha ha ha.

Sorry. I didn't mean to get carried away. But those early surgical experiments were some of the few pleasant times in an otherwise depressing period in my life. Nobody believed in me, I wasn't having any success with my experiments and anything that produced a few laughs was a welcome relief.

Although I did finally perfect the surgical technique to stop farting permanently I came to the realization that if those poor little white mice has anything to say about it they would have opted for a more pleasant method. So with your best interests in mind, I have eliminated this very effective procedure from my 10 day program. (It really burns me up, though, to think I spent all those wasted months sewing up mice fannies. Don't laugh! Have you ever sewed up a mouse's fanny? Well it's no fun but I suppose if all of that research would have panned out I wouldn't feel so bad.)

HYPNOTISM
An aid to stop farting

Hypnotism has proved to be a very effective device for reducing the pain and suffering due to the effects of farting, *once the hypnotism takes place.*

Although I was aware that hypnotism had been used successfully for years to help people stop smoking, I almost failed to experiment with this technique for my flatulence studies because I couldn't figure out a way to get all those white mice to stand still while I swung a watch back and forth in front of their little faces.

But once I solved that problem I soon discovered that hypnotism worked amazingly well with my little non-human test subjects. It was only when I progressed to experimenting with humans that the flaw in my theory surfaced.

Hypnotism takes over the mind of the subject and allows the power of suggestion to overcome even natural bodily functions. One simply hypnotizes the subject and repeats over and over something like, "You will not sneeze" or "You will not be able to hear loud sounds", and Presto!! you can stop your subject from doing just about anything you want.

HOW HYPTNOTISM DOESN'T WORK

Hypnotism sounded so simple. I don't know how I could be so stupid as to not take into consideration one very important element. But I was soon to learn the major flaw in my logic.

First I hypnotized my subjects. Then I repeated my demands over and over and, sure enough, they followed my instructions to the letter. I was sure I had solved the problem but I didn't think ahead and failed to forsee what would happen when I took the experiment out of the laboratory and into the real world.

I had three subjects in my lab for the test: a young gentleman with "the problem", his attractive wife Betty and his mother-in-law, Mrs. Molktwip. They all desperately hoped he could break his habit. So I began to put my brilliant theory to work and hypnotized Betty and Mrs. Molktwip as I repeated over and over, "You will not be able to smell a fart."

And it worked! I asked the gentleman to determine whether or not the test had worked and he began a barrage of tremendous gas bursts which continued until the wallpaper in my lab began to peel. And when the cloud cleared I couldn't believe my eyes; there was no reaction whatsoever from the other two test subjects!! Success?? Well, as I said, the experiment worked in the lab but it wasn't until I started to look ahead to the real world that I realized what I had overlooked.

It suddenly dawned on me that even if I could teach the subject to handle the hypnosis himself, how could he possible hypnotise everyone he came in contact with all day long? I could picture him walking down a busy street, swinging his watch to and fro, as he shouted to everyone within range, "You will not be able to smell...".

No, the hypnosis experiment didn't work but I can't rid myself of the nagging doubt that I just didn't handle it right.

YOU WILL NOT BE ABLE TO SMELL....

LET'S STOP FARTING
Getting Started

Because of the failure of everything from burning at the stake to surgery and hypnotism, most of my colleagues gave up on the study of flatulence and moved on to easier work like looking for a cure for cancer.

But I perservered. So let's proceed to the fruits of my studies: the Poltweed 10 day method.

If you are one of my serious readers and have actually been reading the text thus far, (instead of just looking at the pictures) you've undoubtedly been wondering when the heck I was going to get around to explaining my soon-to-be-famous-10-day-program.

I want to make it perfectly clear that if you think the first part of this book is just "filler" you are sadly mistaken. You don't just jump into something as complex and emotionally draining as my 10 day program without setting the stage, as they say. Trust me. I didn't go through thousands of white mice over the past few years without learning a thing or two. No siree!!

And one of the most important lessons I learned wasn't even when I was in medical school but during my undergraduate years. It was a little tidbit I picked up in Marketing 101:

> "People tend to judge the value
> of a product by its size and
> weight and not always by its value".

So it's really your own fault that you have to plow through 40 or 50 pages of my rambling before you get to the good stuff. If I had simply set down the wisdom I gained over the years on 5 or 6 sheets of paper and hawked them on the street corner, you probably wouldn't have paid more than a buck. MAX.

Well, anyway, here it is. After the big build-up it's time to unveil the secrets behind my fool-proof system. The preceding pages should have taught you 1) I'm qualified, 2) It probably won't work anyhow, 3) You're taking your life in your own hands and, 4) You don't really have a chance in hell of getting your money back. But don't let all of that bother you, you've gone this far...don't stop now!

"Now anyone can stop farting in just 10 days with my new program or their money back!!"

—Dr. H.K. Poltweed

THE POLTWEED 10 DAY METHOD
(A Methodical Approach)

During my studies I made one simple breakthrough which lead to my ultimate success. It was the discovery that farting is such an intense and psychologically gratifying experience that no single anti-fart technique can solve the problem. A change in diet was only partially successful, mechanical and psychological means work sometimes but nothing by itself was a foolproof method. I learned that only a combination of methods, when used together, was successful. Eureka! The Poltweed 10 Day Program was born!!

I have created a program based on three separate but equal elements: dietary recommendations, mechanical devices and psychological aids. Each is equally important. The instructions for each section which follows should be followed to the letter for optimum results.

PHASE I : Diet (Days 1-3)

By now you're all probably expecting the worst. You think I'm going to ruin your life by telling you, "NO MORE BEER! NO MORE PIZZA! NO MORE BRUSSEL SPROUTS!"

Well do I have a pleasant surprise for you. Not only does my 10 day program allow you to *continue* with you traditional well-balanced diet but you will, in fact, be encouraged to consume even larger quantities of your favorite gas producing foods! You see, I am attacking you problem not at its origin (the stomach) but at its intended conclusion.

BREAKFAST:
Please eat lightly and give your stomach a chance to settle down.

LUNCH: (This is the key meal)
        3 hard boiled eggs
        14 slices pizza with sausage/onions
        9 large bags brussel sprouts
        172 cans black beans
        Lite beer at your discretion (but no
        less than 4 six-packs)

Quickly now. . .before the chemical reaction
begins. . .continue on and consume:

        9 tubes SuperGlue
        4 gallons water
        6 lbs. sand
        3 small bags Redi-Mix concrete

If you are at all perceptive you will begin to
realize that this diet will not stop your system
from creating gas. It simply prevents it from
being released into the atmosphere where it
could be offensive to others.

DINNER
Usually the dinner following the Poltweed
special lunch will be a choice between two soft
entrees and jello or ice cream for dessert. A
nice lady in a white uniform and hat will come
around and ask for your selection.

PHASE II: Mechanical Devices (Day 4)

Although the common cork appeared to be a natural as a fart supressant and, in the end, the Cork Technique was perfected, it was finally determined to be too demeaning for everyday use.

Therefore the Poltweed methods utilizes the famed Gas Enhancer Unit. This device has been designed to be worn comfortably about the head so that the main unit dangles in the "line of fire" As gas enters the front of the unit it is enhanced, amplified, and expanded as it rushes out the rear of the unit at 27 times the normal velocity and at twice the normal size.

"Why", you are probably asking yourself, "does the brilliant Dr. Poltweed wish to *increase* the impact of my farts when he says he wants to help me stop?" The answer, Dear Reader, is simple: just a few of these amplified gas bursts in public will be enough to teach you never to fart again. Test results have shown that subjects fart an average of twice while wearing this device. after which they are generally beaten to a bloody pulp,

take four weeks to recover in the nearest hopsital and vow never to fart again.

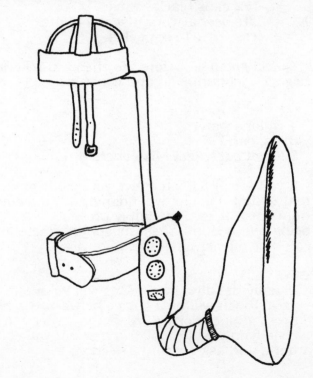

PHASE III : Psychological aids (days 5-10)

"Hey, four eyes! Hey, pizza face! Hey, fatso!" Remember what great fun it was to taunt our less fortunate classmates? Not only was it great fun but this kind of psychological torture was effective as well and has therefore become the "shame factor" portion of my 10 day program.

By this time you have probably accepted the fact that you can't break this habit by yourself. You need help form others, and it is Phase III of my program which allows others to give you this help. In other words, the objective of this exercise is to humiliate you beyond belief and lower your self esteem to the point where you will stop farting, merely to regain your self respect.

To implement the easiest, yet most terrifying part of my program it is necessary to purchase three small items from the Poltweed Institute:
1) A bumper sticker which reads "Farter On Board, No Tailgating".
2) A small sign to be taped to your back reading, "Kick Me If I Fart". And,

3) A colorful button which should be affixed to your lapel which reads, "Don't Let Me Eat Brussel Sprouts".

Now you're probably saying to yourself, "This guy Poltweed is nuts if he thinks I'm going to walk around and broadcast the fact that I fart on occasion! I've spent my entire life trying to hide the fact that I let a little one sneak out

occasionally. I don't want everyone to know that I'm the cause of that rank odor they're smelling!"

Well, dear reader, if I may refer you back to the beginning of this book. Remember... the point I was making is you have not been fooling anyone. You just think you have. And Phase III will simply help you bridge the gap between self deception and self humiliation.

There. That's all there is. The complete Poltweed method. What? You thought there would be a little more to it? Well, if you were foolish enough to have expected more, don't feel bad. You certainly can't feel as foolish as the person who bought this book for you. Just close your eyes and picture how they must have felt walking up to the cash register in a crowded book store while the clerk yells out, "Hey, Joe, we sold another of the books about how to stop farting in 10 days."

Talk about humiliation!

NOW THAT YOU'VE STOPPED
(Are you ready to rejoin society?)

Now that you have stopped, you will note some very wonderful changes begin to take over your body and soul. Not only will you notice an immediate sense of well being but you will become immensely happy, your zits will disappear, hair will begin to fill-in that bald spot and, best of all, your social life will improve rapidly and dramatically.

But that's nothing!

The difference you will really notice is that you will have brought immediate (and, I might add, long over due) relief and happiness to sixty-two (62) other people! Now I know you find it hard to believe that you have been offending that many people with your habit but that's exactly what statistics show. But now is not the time to look back. No need to lament the fact that you used to offend 62 people. Think positively. Now you are bringing happiness to 62 others.

I hate to digress (but I just have to tell you about how excited I got when I ran across the "one farter annoys 62 others" figure.

It occurred to me that, if every time I help one person to stop I make 62 people happy then if I help 10 people stop that makes 620 people happy! What a feeling of power that gave me to know that I, the little pimply face kid who was voted less than likely to succeed, could ultimately be responsible for the happiness of millions of people!!

I hate to admit it because now I realize how stupid I was, but I actually believed I could be responsible, nay revered, for being the genius who made every person in the United States happy!! I calculated that if I could just get 4 million people to stop (x62) then every one of the 230 million people in this country would be happy. (And one person would be *really* happy because he'd be getting the royalties on 4 million books)

But something about my calculations just didn't make sense. At first I couldn't figure out the flaw in my logic but suddenly I figured it out. If only 4 million people stopped that wouldn't make everyone happy because if everyone was happy that would

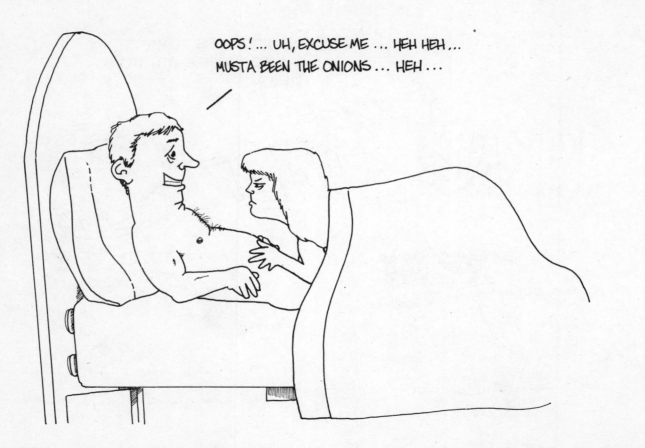

mean nobody was farting. And I was positive there were more than 4 million people in this country farting If I may quote from the widely read and immensely popular I LOVE TO FART COOKBOOK, by Travis Pacone:

"Everyone farts. Even Walter Cronkite."

The following diagrams should help you better understand the basic flaw in my reasoning:

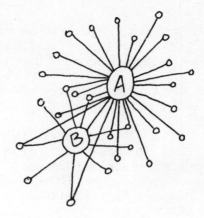

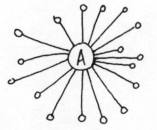

I INCORRECTLY ASSUMED
If individual "A" stopped farting he would make the 62 people around him happy.

WHAT I FAILED TO TAKE INTO CONSIDERATION WAS
What if one of those 62 people was a farter too? Even if individual "A" stops, he doesn't necessarily make those 62 people happy, because if one of them farts, "B", he makes 62 people unhappy and then everything starts to get all confusing.

Boy was I depressed. If Mr. Pacone was right, and *everyone* does fart then the only way to make all of those 62 people happy is for all of them to stop.

And the only way to make everyone in the country happy is for everyone to stop.

I had to face facts that the chance of that happening was pretty slim. But, being the eternal optimist, I didn't stay depressed for long. Maybe it was a long shot but if it ever did happen, I'd be sitting on the royalities from over 200 million books!!

CREDIT WHERE CREDIT IS DUE
Many Thanks to My Thousands of "Volunteers"

I've received more than my share of fame and fortune over the past year as the result of my revolutionary 10 day program. But I refuse to take all of the credit. I would be remiss if I didn't use this forum to give special thanks to the thousands of little fellows (and gals) who were invaluable to my studies.

Over 36,000 of those fuzzy little friends passed through my laboratory over the past few years. Actually I became quite close to many of them (and this was exceedingly difficult considering the diets I had devised for them). Unlike the relatively few human volunteers I utilized, these cute little creatures never complained, argued or talked back. And most of them seemed to truly enjoy their special diets.

Of course it was necessary that a few of my little mousie friends "pass away" in the interest of scientific discovery and this fact I truly lament. But as Louis Pasteur used to say,"Hey, mon ami...some things got to die when you're doing le experiment and it's better if they're mice than guys like you and me." Honest, he really said that.

THE TRUE CULPRIT
(An Essay on Brussel Sprouts)

We all know that Brussels is the capital of Belguim just as we all know that Belgian people fart more than anyone else in the world. The question is, why?

Well, you certainly won't find the answer to this profound question in any Belgian history book. To find the facts it's necessary to look into the history of England where the true story is told.

In 729 A.D., just after the Celts defeated the Moors in the battle of Waterloo, England was not an island as it is today but was attached to Belgium (see map). It was around this time that the English invented beer-making and their economy was booming. Belguim, however, was an extremely poor country with no agriculture or heavy industry. Although they had started making waffles, it was simply not enough.

The King of Belgium decreed that farmers should plant the recently discovered Chinese vegetable, the Brussel Sprout. His advisors told him this would revive the economy, put everyone to work and become a major cash crop for the country. Soon the entire Belgian countryside was planted with sprouts, and farmers were making tons of money. The nation's capital changed it's name from Cleveland to Brussels in trubute to this new economic miracle and everyone seemed happy.

Everyone, that is, except the Belgian's next door neighboors, the English who were rapidly becoming concerned about the new air pollution resulting from excess consumption of the new crop.

You see, after the Belgians planted the sprouts they also began to eat them. Soon all two million inhabitants of Belguim were eating brussel sprouts for breakfast, lunch, and dinner. The result, as anyone who has ever eaten a brussel sprout knows, was a dramatic increase in flatulence throughout the entire country.

Obviously, as huge clouds of foul smelling gas continued to drift over their country, the English became enraged. Finally they hired 257,000 Chinese coolies to dig a trench the length of their border with Belgium, and rowed their new island to a safe distance, 60 miles off shore, where they anchored it securely.

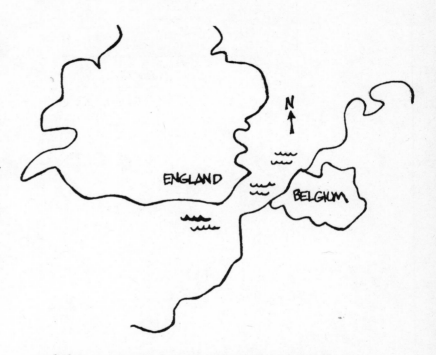

The Belgians, although embarassed by this chain of events, continued their harvest of sprouts. In an attempt to hide their reputation from potential tourists they changed the spelling of their capital city to Bruxells and this seems to have worked, because although people still curse the lowly brussel sprout, they tend to forget the part this tiny country played in this important historical event.

ANSWERS TO IMPORTANT QUESTIONS
GENERALLY ASKED BY MY PATIENTS

Q. **When I stop, will I experience withdrawal pains?**

A. I can't believe you people ask this question so frequently? What are you worried about? It's not as if you're breaking a drug habit or if someone is going to rip out your fingernails. Come on, don't be such babies.
Yes

Q. **Is it true that cauliflower causes the most smelly gas in the world?**

A. Without a doubt, no! (This was true as little as three years ago however, at that time, the California Cauliflower Institute donated $10,000 to my research studies. I can now say without a doubt, it is not true. The Brussel Sprout is the culprit.)

Q. **I've heard that if I suppress my farting habit and don't fart for long periods of time, those smelly gasses will build up inside of me and slowly begin to poison my system ultimately causing my organs and especially my skin to smell. Is this true?**

A. I can't be sure. I once assembled a group of volunteers to test this theory but they all quit to become New York cab drivers so I was never able to see the final results of my experiments.

Q. I am concerned about which foods I should eat if I want to cut down on my farting. Can you tell me which foods I should stay away from??

A. I have prepared a chart for you which shows many of the most common foods in order of their danger.

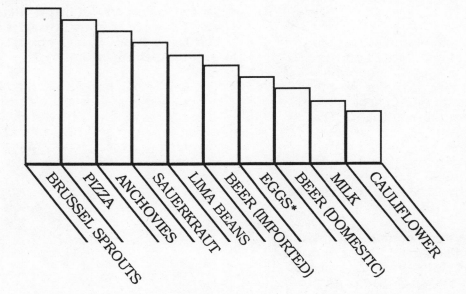

BRUSSEL SPROUTS
PIZZA
ANCHOVIES
SAUERKRAUT
LIMA BEANS
BEER (IMPORTED)
EGGS*
BEER (DOMESTIC)
MILK
CAULIFLOWER

*Authors note: Although eggs do not cause the most flatulence activity, they do have the most horrendous odor imaginable

Q. I attended one of your lectures where you talked about a place where people who simply flat out don't want to stop farting can gather. I can't remember the particulars, can you refresh my memory?

A. Sure. You're talking about the famous Hawaiian Fart Colony. Based on the leper colonies, it is a place where habitual farters can gather and enjoy each other's company in enough seclusion to insure they do not offend others. The Fart Colony is great fun. Guests often sit around the fire at night and watch the Hawaiian volcanoes spew forth foul smelling gasses. One note of caution, however. I've heard it's often too noisy to get to sleep at night.

Q. I've always been very considerate when it comes to my bad habit. Every time I feel the "urge", I politely excuse myself and leave the room until the urge passes (so to speak). What can I do about my friends who think all this coming and going is strange behavior?

A. The best way to handle this problem is to just stick around once when the urge hits. I guarantee they'll never complain again.

Q. Sometimes I sneak out a "little one" and I'm sure it goes unnoticed. Do you think my habit is bad enough that I have to worry about stopping?

A. The key words here are "little one". My experience has shown that one person's idea of little is often powerful enough to melt the doors on Fort Knox. Do everyone a favor...give it up.

Q. **Farting has been more or less a sport in our family for generations. We all seem to enjoy it. Therefore the only reason we would consider stopping is for our neighbor's benefit. Do you think it's worth it just to keep them happy?**

A. Sport? Let me put it this way: until such time that the Internationl Olympic Committe decides to add farting as an official Olympic event I would say it's time to put a halt to your activities. (But don't despair, I hear that bowling is on the schedule for the '88 games, so there's still hope).

Q. **I don't understand what the big deal is about farting. Can you explain it to me?**

A. I'm glad you asked because there are a lot of people like you out there. I've prepared the following graphic information to explain everything clearly.

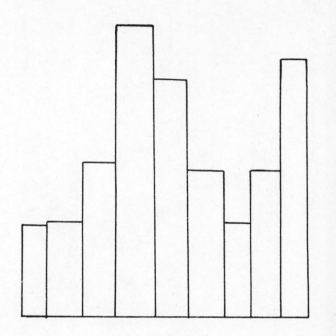

FARTBUSTERS!
For more information dial 1-800-**N-O-F-A-R-T-S**

FARTBUSTERS
Get Rich!

Yes sir! There's money to be made in the anti-farting business and I can prove it. (You're reading this book aren't you? Someone bought this book didn't they? I guess that makes me pretty much of an expert on the profitability of the fart-stopping game).

But, not one to be greedy, I'm going to let all of you in on the secrets of how you, too, can profit from the public's desire to have a sweeter smelling environment.

By purchasing one of my exclusive fartbusters franchises you can take advantage of my years of experience. You'll become an expert overnight just by virtue of your association with the Poltweed name. And here's what else you get:

1) A guaranteed sales and marketing territory of 27.842 square miles in which no other authorized Fartbuster franchise may operate. (Historical note: Most people think 1 meter is "about 3 feet" but actually it is precisely 1 millionth part of the distance from the Equator to the North Pole. Similarly, 27.842 square miles is not just "some randomly selected territory", but precisely the area which would be devastated by 11,111 average people farting all at the same time!)

2) Complete Fartbusters equipment package including official uniform and the instantly recognizable and world famous FB insignia.

3) Comprehensive advertising and promotional support in the form of sample yellow page ads, telephone solicitation scripts and, our most successful promotional tool, 1,000 copies of my famous tract, How to Stop Farting in Ten Days or Your Money Back.

WHO YOU GONNA CALL?

Fart Busters!

CONCLUSION
(Who Really Cares?)

If there is a conclusion to be drawn from all this it is certainly not in the profound nature of the text, nor in the delicate line of the illustration.

No, if one were to draw conclusions from the existence of this small but pithy tomb, it would be that people *do* fart, they sincerely want to stop, but they find it virtually impossible to do so, and...who really *cares* anyway?! (Last season when Mike Wallace did a feature about flatulence on **60 Minutes**, they had the lowest ratings in their history).

We humans love to fart, have always done so and will continue to do so until that one unlucky day, sometime in the future, when the entire human race will, by chance, fart all at the same time and the universe will end, just as some people believe it started, with a big bang.

Available at fine book stores everywhere or order direct from the publisher by using the coupon below.

Blue Frog Publishing Company
44 E. Superior
Chicago, IL 60611

HOW TO STOP FARTING IN 10 DAYS

To order one copy simply enclose $5.95 plus $1.25 shipping and handling. For orders of 5 or more copies, publisher pays all mailing and handling charge.
Illinois residents add 5% state sales tax.

Enclosed is $ _____ plus $_____ shipping and handling.

Please send _____ copies.

Mailing Label ---- Please print clearly

_____

Name

_____

Address

_____

City   State   Zip

OTHER STRANGE AND WONDERFUL HUMOR BOOKS
FROM TURNBULL & WILLOUGHBY

The Nun Book
A Behing-the-Scene Peek $4.95
The One Minute Gynecologist
"Why Do I Have to Go?" $4.95
The Joy of Shopping
Every Woman's Hilarious Companion $4.95
The Jewish AmericanPrincess Handbook
A Jewish HumorClassic $4.95
The Jewish American Prince Handbook
The Princesses Revenge! $5.95
The I Love to Fart Cookbook
It's a Gas! $4.95
The Modern Guide to Sexual Etiquette
Proper Etiquette for ModernLadies and
Gentlemen $5.95
How to Hang a Spoon
(On Your Face) The Ultimate Guide $5.95
Boffo
Can't Be Explained $4.95
The Snuggle Book
The Fine Art of Snuggling $5.95

Available in fine bookstores everywhere or order
direct from the publisher

**Turnbull & Willoughby
Publishers
44 E. Superior
Chicago, IL 60611**

Please ship the following books:

Title   Quantity

_____   _____

_____   _____

_____   _____

_____   _____

name

street

city   state   zip